100 Property Investment Tips:

Learn from the experts and accelerate your success

The Property Hub

Contents

Introduction

Just over two years ago, I was sitting in a hotel room in Bangkok and Rob Bence was at home in Hertfordshire. We flipped on our microphones and recorded the first episode of The Property Podcast - which was one of the more cringeworthy half hours of listening you could ever subject yourself to, but turned out to be the start of something very special.

On the day this book was published, episode number 100 of The Property Podcast was broadcast - having gathered tens of thousands of listeners and over 250 five-star reviews along the way. We've become a little better as presenters over time (although this book should still be dedicated to our editor), but the thing that's made the show such a success is our audience's ceaseless enthusiasm for the subject of property investment.

Why are we so obsessed with property investment that we started a show about it, and why do thousands of others share that enthusiasm? Because it really can change your life - both in a financial sense, and in terms of the knowledge you gain and the people you meet along the road to wealth and financial security. It's our mission to demystify property investment and provide access to knowledge about it as cheaply as possible, for as many people as possible. Because we love it, and we want to share what we know with anyone who'll listen.

It's the enthusiasm of our audience that has pushed us to release an episode of The Property Podcast at 7am every Thursday morning for two years - including Christmas Day and New Year's Day - whatever else is going on in our businesses or personal lives. And it's why we created The Property Hub (www.thepropertyhub.net) - a completely free online community that numbers thousands of members and includes forums, blogs, video courses and live events.

So when we decided to put together a book, it was immediately obvious that we should ask the members of The Property Hub to help us. Because although we're involved in property every single day through RMP Property (www.rmpproperty.com) and Yellow Lettings (www.yellowlettings.net), we've never pretended to know it all - and what makes us so proud of The Property Hub is that it's full of exceptionally smart and generous people, teaching us as well as each other.

In this book you'll find, as the title suggests, 100 tips to help you succeed in property investment - whether you're yet to get started or have been doing it for years. These tips aren't just from us, but from over 30 investors with completely different outlooks, experiences and strategies.

Some you'll already know, some you'll disagree with, some may even contradict each other... but there's no "right" way to invest in property and nobody knows it all, so if you pick up just one new idea from this book we hope you'll consider it worth your while.

After you've enjoyed this book, join us in The Property Hub to fill in any gaps and share what you know. And if you register your purchase of this book at www.thepropertyhub.net/tipsbonus, we've got some more free resources for you that we couldn't fit into the book itself.

Now... on to the tips!

Rob Dix

Chapter 1: Get started

Invest in the fundamentals

When choosing which area to invest in, you need to make sure it has a strong tenant demand - not just now but in the future. How can you do that? By looking at the "fundamentals" of each area.

When assessing an area, look for the following.

- Shops - are they local and plentiful?

- Transport links - are there good road networks, train links and buses?

- Schools - are they local and of a good standard?

- Investment - any future plans?

- Employment - who is likely to employ your tenants?

Don't rely on just one or two of the fundamentals - make sure you look for them all. You *might* be able to find a good deal in Knowhereville, but who will rent it from you?

- Rob Bence, www.thepropertyhub.net/rob-bence

Replicate a model that works

As a successful investor once said to me, there are no prizes for originality in property: if you see a model that works, just nick it and implement it yourself.

Of course, you need to make sure that the model works for you: everyone is different in terms of their skills, attitude to risk, and what they want their day-to-day life to look like. You might see someone who's making a lot of money, but would you be prepared to do what they did to get there? If you see what their life is like now, would you want it for yourself?

In *Beyond The Bricks* (www.thepropertyhub.net/btb), I interviewed nine investors who had all become successful by taking very different approaches. Some had done it in months; others in decades. Some had almost lost it all multiple times along the way; others just plodded safely along. Some were rushing around visiting properties and taking meetings every day; others only got out of their dressing gowns on special occasions.

So have no shame in taking a model that works and making it your own - but first, make sure it's right for you.

- Rob Dix, www.thepropertyhub.net/rob-dix

Don't compare yourself to others

Not everyone is a property millionaire.

Keep YOUR goal in mind. Every property investor/landlord has a different story and started with varying degrees of financial leverage and liquidity. Do NOT compare yourself to them but - whether you decide to be cautious or risky - make your investment actions count.

As long as you're comfortable with your risk, that's all that matters: everything evens itself out in the long run, so don't get greedy and try to beat the "property millionaire" with the flashy car and sharp suit. Real success stories in property don't need to show off - and they know that a Porsche is a stupid car for taking a soiled mattress to the tip, and a posh suit will get ruined while searching for a stop cock underneath the floorboards.

- Serena Thompson, www.thepropertyhub.net/serena-thompson

Account for your time and energy as well as your costs

One of the golden rules of investing in property is to monitor your costs - and to make sure that financially speaking, you get more out of your investment than you put in.

Property costs are calculated in more ways than one, though. Each property you own will take some of your time – to source, purchase, rent out, etc. – and some of your energy. Some will have higher "costs" than others. Is the financial return worth the time and energy cost? You can get money back, but never your time or energy.

- **Jayne Owen,** www.thepropertyhub.net/jayne-owen

Love good debt; hate bad debt

What's the difference between "good" debt (known as "leverage") and "bad" debt?

Generally speaking, good debt is used to buy an appreciating asset where the interest payments are covered by the income generated from that asset. Bad debt is a loan used to buy a depreciating asset that does not generate any income.

Let's say Bill wants to save for the deposit on a flat and Ben wants to buy a new car. They both have £300 per month available to use. Bill invests his £300 per month in an equity ISA, giving an average annual income and capital growth of 10% combined. Ben buys a car costing £300 per month, which includes the finance charges.

After six years, Bill has accrued a tax-free lump sum of around £30,000 in his ISA. He uses it as the deposit on a flat costing £100,000, and obtains a buy-to-let mortgage to cover the balance of £70,000.

Ben has paid off his car loan: his car is now only worth about £10,000.

Nine years later and Bill's flat has increased in value by the historical average of 9% per year, which means it's now worth £200,000 - double the value when he bought it. Over the past nine years he's used the rental income profit to pay down his mortgage debt by £10,000 - leaving him with mortgage debt of £60,000 and £140,000 of equity in the property.

Ben's car is now 15 years old and he's just had it towed away to the scrap yard, as it has no value left at all.

- Graeham Broderick

Network with other investors

As an introvert, the idea of "networking" brings me out in a cold sweat: I associate it with name badges, fear, and being backed slowly into a corner while someone aggressively pitches me on whatever it is that they do.

In reality, networking doesn't have to be like that: it's a great way to increase your success in property, and (I can't believe I'm saying this) it can even be fun.

Having a network means having people who can put deals your way, who can recommend the best professionals to work with, and to whom you can turn when you've got any kind of problem. My own network has created tens of thousands of pounds for me in opportunities created and costs saved - and building that network hasn't even felt like work.

The Property Hub holds regular in-person events around the UK, and our members arrange smaller meetups of their own in between - they're guaranteed to be friendly, informal, and with no sales pitches whatsoever. Still, you don't have to go to any kind of event: just find an investor you admire and offer to buy them lunch in exchange for a chat. Most investors are happy to talk about what they do and share advice.

And of course, you can network without leaving the house at all: The Property Hub is a non-stop online networking event, and you can also link up with fellow investors on Twitter,

Facebook and LinkedIn.

Want help in getting started? Register your purchase of this book at www.thepropertyhub.net/tipsbonus, and we'll send you a Twitter list of some of the most interesting property investors to follow - just follow the whole list with one click, and that's your network started!

- Rob Dix, www.thepropertyhub.net/rob-dix

Trust, but validate

Property investing can be a minefield: to make a decision you have to collate a lot of information, process it and take action.

The challenge is that much of the information you need is provided by third parties: mortgage brokers, letting agents, property sourcers, etc. It's important to build great relationships with these people, but how do you know who to trust?

Instinct is a great starting point, but it's not enough: if your instincts deceive you and you make a decision based on incorrect information, your once-brilliant investment becomes a dud.

So it's important to also validate all key information that's provided to you. Here are some ways in which you can do that:

- Check all information independently by researching for yourself. For example, if someone tells you that a property will rent for £500 a month, go on Rightmove and check similar properties.

- Get a second opinion. For example, if an estate agent tells you that a property will rent brilliantly, call someone else who's not trying to sell you something and see what they have to say about it.

- Search online for any information about people you're dealing with, to see if anything negative has been written about them.

When you've validated the information, you're in a better place to trust those third parties and invest with confidence.

- **Rob Bence, <u>www.thepropertyhub.net/rob-bence</u>**

Use net yield instead of gross yield

The simplest way to calculate rental yield is to divide a property's price by the yearly rent - giving you an amount that's known as the "gross yield". But this is the wrong indictor or KPI to use - and when someone talks about yield in terms of gross yield, you can tell they're not an experienced landlord.

Gross yield doesn't take into account any of the costs associated with owning a property - such as the mortgage and the ongoing spending on maintenance, insurance, service charges, letting agent fees, etc.

Once these costs have been factored in, you end up with "net yield". Calculating the net yield is a far more practical - not to mention realistic - way of determining how much your property is making you.

- John Corey, www.thepropertyhub.net/john-corey

Use leverage to multiply your returns

Leverage acts like a lever: by applying a small force at one end, you can produce a bigger force at the other. And the longer the lever, the bigger the amplification effect. In the case of property investment, the small force you put in is your deposit, and the lever is the mortgage.

A mortgage (the leverage) can multiply your returns many times over compared to using pure cash to buy a property. Here's how it works:

Let's say Bill and Ben each inherited £100,000 from their parents, and they both wanted to invest the money in buy-to-let property.

- Bill bought a flat for £100,000 cash.

- Ben bought four £100,000 flats by dividing his money into four £25,000 deposits and getting four buy-to-let mortgages for £75,000 to make up the balances.

The flats were all let out for £450 per month.

- Bill saved his monthly profit after expenses of £350.

- Ben had to pay mortgage interest on his loans, so he

saved £100 per month.

After nine years of property prices rising at an average 9% a year…

- Bill's flat is worth £200,000, which means he's increased the value of his investment by £100,000. He's also made £37,800 from saving up £350 a month for nine years. In total, the value of his initial £100,000 investment is £237,800.

- Ben's four flats increased in value at the same rate as Bill's and are now worth £800,000 in total. He saved £10,800 from saving up £100 a month. After deducting the four mortgages (£300,000), Ben's investment is now worth £510,800.

Because Ben used leverage to buy his flats, he increased the value of his investment by £273,000 more than his brother Bill.

Looking forward another 20 years (assuming the same level of average price rises and assuming rents rise by 50% after each ten-year period to simplify matters)…

- Bill's flat is now worth £800,000 and he's saved £170,000 in rental profits, giving him a total investment value of £970,000.

- Ben's four flats are now worth £3,200,000, and he's

saved £48,000 in rental profits. After deducting his
four mortgages he has £2,948,000 of equity and cash.

Ben's investment has increased by more than three times that
of his brother. To multiply his returns by even more than this,
Ben could have remortgaged his four flats every few years and
withdrawn equity to use as deposits on even more properties.

- Graeham Broderick

Understand the power of compounding

The definition of compounding is: "The ability of an asset to generate earnings, which are then reinvested in order to generate their own earnings."

To understand the power of compounding is to understand THE most powerful tool of wealth creation. If you haven't ever done so before, I urge you to sit down with a piece of paper, a pencil and a calculator. Now multiply your original investment by the percentage you predict it to grow by over the course of a year, and then repeat the process for every year you intend to hold that asset.

Let's assume you believe that the property market will continue to grow annually, on average, at a rate of 9% - as it has done since records began.

- You've bought a flat for £100,000 with a £25,000 deposit.

- After one year the flat is worth 9% more and has therefore increased in value by £9,000 to £109,000.

- After two years it has increased in value by 9% again - this time on top of the new value of £109,000 - meaning the flat is now worth £118,810 - £9,810 more than last year.

- Repeat this process for however long you intend to hold the asset for. Let's say 30 years. After 30 years an asset originally worth £100,000 compounding at an average annual rate of 9% could be worth in the region of £1,470,000.

Have fun with that calculator!

- Graeham Broderick

Invest in yourself first

Just as a lack of oxygen to the brain is the only thing that will technically kill a person, a lack of cash in the bank is the only thing that will technically kill a rental property business. So as property investors, ultimately we live or die through our cashflow.

Cashflow can be protected in two ways - and both stem from knowledge.

- The first is to know how to take appropriate care of a rental property to avoid cashflow-sapping void periods.

- The second is to educate ourselves about the principles of leverage, compound growth and inflation - which can be very powerful, but also dangerous if used incorrectly.

As a result, it's best to start investing in ourselves before investing in any properties - and that investment in skills, knowledge and mindset is the best you can possibly make.

- Richard Brown, <u>www.thepropertyhub.net/richard-brown</u>

Don't spend a fortune on property education

When the property market is booming, you'll find plenty of courses promising to educate you about property investment. Often the initial event will be cheap or free, with an "upsell" to an expensive course where you'll learn the "real" secrets.

In truth, there are no real secrets - you can learn almost everything you need to know cheaply (starting with the resources we recommend in this book) or from experience.

This isn't to say that all courses are useless: there's a motivational benefit, and there are excellent courses on specific aspects of property investment taught by experts in their field. But don't feel like you'll miss out on any secrets if you choose the cheap or free route - there's still an endless amount you can learn, and you'll have more in the bank for your next deposit.

- Rob Dix, www.thepropertyhub.net/rob-dix

Don't go alone - build a team

Property investment requires so many different skills - financing, sourcing, strategy, conveyancing and DIY to name a few - and chances are you're not an expert at every discipline! That's why it's important to build a team: you can focus on doing what you're good at, and you can leave other people to do the rest. Your team should be able to save you time and money, and help you to accelerate your success.

Depending on your strategy, you should look to have most of the following people in your team:

- Mortgage broker

- Solicitor

- Sourcer (company or individual)

- Mentor (this can be a formal or informal)

- Handyman or builder

Consider asking for referrals to give you peace of mind that you're picking the right people. And feel free to contact me if you're in need of some recommended team members!

- Rob Bence, www.thepropertyhub.net/rob-bence

Consider the alternatives to buy-to-let

Property investing isn't limited to buy-to-let and do-up-and-sell transactions. If you believe in property as an asset class - and that it has unique attributes which can benefit you as an investor - you should consider some of the alternatives.

Property funds, which come in various forms, offer access to commercial property investment in a way that's more liquid (easily accessible) and where the risk is shared between all the investors in the fund. They come in various forms such as OEICs and Unit Trusts, Real-Estate Investment Trusts (REITs) and the newer Property Authorised Investment Funds (PAIFs).

Despite the confusing acronyms, they largely do the same thing. You can invest in these funds within an ISA for capital gains tax benefits.

If you haven't yet amassed enough for a deposit on a buy-to-let, or if you want to diversify away from bricks-and-mortar property investing, property funds are worth considering.

- Pete Matthew, www.thepropertyhub.net/pete-matthew

Take calculated risks

Do you ever hear or read about people who became very successful by working their socks off for someone else eight hours a day, five days a week until they retired at 65 - having taken just four weeks' holiday a year and put every spare penny they earned into their pension and savings accounts?

Investing in anything - whether it be a business, property or shares - involves a certain amount of risk. Generally speaking, the fewer risks you take in life, the lower and more predictable the returns and vice versa.

"To take no risk is the greatest risk." I have no idea who said this, but I agree with it. Taking small, calculated risks throughout one's life generally leads to rewarding returns.

Imagine if you hadn't asked your partner to dance, even though at the time the risk of rejection by the most beautiful girl you'd ever seen was almost too much to deal with. What's the worst that could have happened if she'd declined? Maybe a red face and a little disappointment?

Imagine driving past that flat you'd thought of buying 30 years ago for £100,000. It's now worth £800,000 and rents out for £5,000 a month. At the time you'd have only required a £25,000 deposit, yet you didn't buy it because you read something negative about property in a newspaper and decided to buy a new car instead (which went on the scrap heap 15 years ago).

If you really think about anything that you or someone else has achieved, however great or small, it will usually be due to the fact that some kind of risk was taken. Whether you're a footballer taking the risk of passing to another player or shooting for goal yourself, a doctor making a life-or-death decision in an A&E ward, or an entrepreneur starting a new business, risk is involved in the outcome.

If you're worried about the risk of doing something, ask yourself: "What's the worst that can happen if I do this? And what's the best that can happen if I do this?" Weigh everything up and decide whether it's worth the risk or not...

- Graeham Broderick

Make sure you know why property goes up in value

History shows that UK property prices rise over time and, on average, they actually double in value every nine years. What causes this to happen, and will it continue?

Many factors have pushed property prices up over the years, but there's one huge driving force: supply and demand. Or more specifically, lack of supply and too much demand.

In 1994, a government report (Barker Report) looked at the housing crisis and concluded that we needed to build 250,000 new homes each year. Since then, we've failed to hit that figure even once. In fact, most of the time we don't even build half that many.

Today - as the population continues to grow - that target needs to be revised upwards, and some reports now suggest that we need to build over 300,000 homes each year. But we're still nowhere near building that many! It's no wonder that property prices continue to rise as a result.

This is not a new phenomenon: since the 1950s we've experienced a lack of supply and increased demand.

So what can we do with this information? Take confidence in the fact that unless something very dramatic happens,

property prices will continue to rise in the long term. Yes ,
sometimes property *does* fall in value, but history has taught us
that it recovers to rise again.

- **Rob Bence,** www.thepropertyhub.net/rob-bence

Form a mastermind group

A mastermind group is a small number of people - usually about four to six - who regularly get together to hold each other accountable and support each other to reach their goals.

The advantages of being part of a mastermind group are twofold. Firstly, it's useful to push you to take action: when life gets in the way and you're tempted to let your property activities slide, you're less likely to do so if you know you'll need to make a lame excuse in front of your group next week! Secondly, it's beneficial to get an outside perspective on what you're trying to achieve. Good ideas can come from anywhere - and others will often have contacts, suggestions or tips from experience that you never would have come up with on your own.

We dedicated a whole episode of The Property Podcast to telling you exactly how to set up your own mastermind group. We also hold a quarterly in-person mastermind-style strategy day (called The Property Hub Summit) for a small group of investors who want to get guidance from us and their peers.

You'll find links to both (along with many other goodies) in the **bonus resources**. Just register your purchase of this book at www.thepropertyhub.net/tipsbonus to access them all.

- **Rob Dix, www.thepropertyhub.net/rob-dix**

Educate yourself while you're out driving or jogging!

Podcasts are a great way to fit learning about any subject into what would otherwise be "dead time" - on your commute, at the gym...we've even had people tell us they've listened while feeding the baby or clearing out the gutters!

The Property Hub puts out four podcasts every single week:

- **The Property Podcast** (www.thepropertyhub.net/podcast) is our flagship weekly show, now with over 100 episodes. Every week we discuss the news, share a new resource and choose a property-related topic to talk about.

- **Property Investment Tips** (www.thepropertyhub.net/podcast) is like this book in audio form, designed to expose you to an important new property idea in under ten minutes. No chit-chat - just property tips from us and our team of guest experts. It's perfect for when you've just got a little bit of spare time.

- **Property News Radio** (www.thepropertyhub.net/pnr) is also short and to-the-point, rounding up the important news stories of the week in just 15 minutes.

- And finally, **The Property Geek Podcast** (www.thepropertyhub.net/pgp) dives deeper into a certain area of property investment every week, often with the help of a special guest with specific expertise.

Never listened to a podcast before, and not sure how to? Don't worry! Register your purchase of this book at www.thepropertyhub.net/tipsbonus and you'll find a complete guide to how to subscribe to our podcasts, so that each episode gets automatically downloaded to your phone or iPod.

- Rob Dix, www.thepropertyhub.net/rob-dix

Start as young as possible

When we did our Big Property Investor Survey in 2014 (www.thepropertyhub.net/surveyresults2014), we asked them what one piece of advice they wish they'd received before starting. And a third of investors said they wish they'd been advised to start younger.

Start as early as you can. Property investment is a meritocracy: no one will judge you for being young. And the more years you have for your returns to compound, the more money you'll have in the end.

- **Rob Dix, www.thepropertyhub.net/rob-dix**

Find the confidence to take the first step onto the property ladder

Step 1: Buy a notebook to jot down everything to do with your property journey. Being able to look back over tips, property prices, estate agents, contact details, etc. makes life so much easier. You can do this electronically of course, but there's something very satisfying about having it all in a special book.

Step 2: Listen to as many episodes of The Property Podcast as possible (starting at number 1) before buying your first property. Listening to it while ironing or having breakfast is great, but always keep your notebook by your side: writing down key points as you hear them helps to clarify them in your mind. The show on leverage (episode 18 - www.thepropertyhub.net/leverageexplained) is one of the most helpful for a newbie! Once you've listened to several episodes, your confidence and knowledge will hopefully have increased enough to make that first purchase.

- Jane Nimmo

Chapter 2: Find a deal

Buy below market value

If you want to be successful in property investment, you have to adhere to my most important rule: always buy below market value!

The ability to buy below market value (BMV) is one of the reasons why property investment appeals to me over other investment classes. You can't go into a bank and negotiate an ISA rate, and you can't ask a stockbroker to sell you shares below their market value… but you CAN do that with property!

Buying BMV can accelerate your success and make a huge difference to how quickly you can build your portfolio. Here's an example to show how:

When you buy a property, your mortgage lender will only lend based on the purchase price - not its market value. So if they're willing to make you a loan at 75% loan-to-value and you buy a house for £150,000, they'll give you £112,500 and you'll have to put in £37,500 of your own money - even if you secured a discount of 25% and the property was really worth £200,000.

However, when you've owned the property for six months, you can remortgage with a different lender - and this time they'll lend based on the market value rather than the purchase price.

What does this mean? Well, you put in £37,500 of your own cash, and six months later you move to a new lender who'll extend your borrowing by £37,500. That goes straight into your bank account, so you've got your entire deposit back - ready to use on your next purchase.

Meanwhile, the total borrowing against your original purchase is now £150,000. The market value is £200,000, so you've still got 25% equity!

It's not easy to negotiate on investment property prices - and it may require some help from a professional property sourcer - but it's worth spending time on finding out how.

- Rob Bence, www.thepropertyhub.net/rob-bence

Transport links are key

When I bought my first property for my daughter at Chelsea College of Art, she was a typical lazy teenager - and I knew she wouldn't bother going into college unless it was as easy as pie to get there! So I drew a circle around the area and made sure there were extensive transport links in the area. It worked: she went to college and now she's a successful freelance graphic designer doing great!

My point is that transport links are key! Everyone in London wants to fall out of bed and get to work. A maximum ten-minute walk to any station was my goal. It's worked for me ever since: now I have eight properties in London.

- Helen Garvey

Keep looking - even after you've had an offer accepted

If I could go back in time and give myself some advice, it would be: "Keep looking." Even after getting an offer accepted, keep looking and looking because anything can happen.

It's no fun to be in a situation where a property falls through and you've wasted two months waiting for it to happen. My first investment experience was like that, and I wasted so much time just waiting! The second time I decided to invest, I was more prepared - so when the property fell through, I already had another one lined up!

- Daniel Tracey

Research, research, research

Research, research, research!

You need to research whether your desired location will satisfy the tenant group you want to attract. And is there demand within that tenant group for the type of property you want to buy? And is that type of property available to buy in your desired location?

It all requires research!

- Phil Stewardson, <u>www.thepropertyhub.net/phil-stewardson</u>

Get a valuation report for a fraction of the price

If you're trying to asses if a deal is below market value (BMV), you may want to get a valuation report done. Instructing a valuer can be expensive, but there's another option: a desktop valuation report.

Used by four of the five biggest UK banks, Hometrack (www.thepropertyhub.net/hometrack) also allows the general public to access its services. Answer a few basic questions about the property you're researching and it will produce a comprehensive report on the property in question. The cost is less than £25 - great value for the confidence it can give you in your decision.

- Rob Bence, www.thepropertyhub.net/rob-bence

Look for unmortgageable properties

If you often find yourself priced out by other buyers who're prepared to pay more than you think a property is worth... here's a solution: find properties that aren't mortgageable!

There are many reasons why lenders won't offer a mortgage on a property. For example:

- It doesn't have a kitchen or bathroom.

- It has a short lease (typically less than 70 years).

- It has been built using unusual materials.

- It is derelict or in severe disrepair.

- It's close to an area where there's been recent flooding.

There's far less competition for such properties, so you have a pretty clear field. The trick is to buy them, refurbish them (or do whatever else needs to be done) to make them mortgageable, then sell them on or refinance to realise your profit.

If you don't have the cash to buy without a mortgage, you can also make use of "bridging finance" - a short-term funding option that has fewer restrictions than regular mortgages.

- **Kevin Wright,** www.thepropertyhub.net/kevin-wright

Keep tabs on every property

I viewed a property, I liked the property, I made an offer. The offer was rejected, so I made a slightly higher offer - which was also rejected.

I was deflated, but didn't want to go any higher.

A month later I noticed that the property was still being advertised, and - because I knew via Property Bee that a sale had fallen through the year before - I thought I'd try to chat to the estate agent about it. (Find out more about Property Bee in Chapter 7.)

I told the estate agent that I was still interested, but I didn't want to waste his time if the seller was intent on achieving a price that was completely out of line with the property's value. The agent let me know what he thought the seller would accept. I suggested that I'd meet the seller halfway - which was just £2,000 more than my previous offer.

And… the offer was accepted!

Had I not kept my eye on the property and given the agent a call, I'd have missed out on the deal.

- Kylie Ackers, <u>www.thepropertyhub.net/kylie-ackers</u>

Get a letting agent's opinion on a potential purchase

When you're considering a potential buy-to-let purchase, find out from a local letting agent what rent it will achieve and how quickly it's likely to be snapped up by a tenant. Here's how:

In Rightmove, check properties for rent near your target property and see which agent seems to have the biggest local presence. Call up, tell them you're considering buying something in the area and want a rough guide as to what it could achieve, and tell them key details like the street it's on and how many bedrooms it has.

The agent will then be able to go through similar properties on their books and tell you what they're rented out for. Ask the agent how quickly they tend to get rented, and what the factors are that separate the ones that rent quickly from the ones that stick; often it's just quality and price, but there might be other things that you can watch out for.

If you're honest with the agent about it only being a potential purchase at this stage, they have no motivation to give you anything but honest advice.

- **Rob Dix, www.thepropertyhub.net/rob-dix**

Always meet the valuer at the property

If you're buying a property with a mortgage, it's always a good idea to find out the date and time of the valuation and then go to meet the valuer. You'll be able to answer any questions they might have, and - if necessary - inform them about your plans for the property.

I've learnt from experience! I recently had an offer accepted on a property, and a valuation was completed in my absence. The valuer classed the property as an HMO because of a few internal locks and an electric cooker wired into one of the bedrooms - even though sufficient safety measures weren't in place for it to actually **be** an HMO (wired smoke alarms, electric lighting, etc.), and the property wasn't registered with the City Council as an HMO in a qualifying area.

I shared my experience with other investors, and many of them informed me that they always meet the valuer at the property to avoid situations like this. It's a practice I'll definitely adopt in the future: I'm sure it will save a lot of time and heartache!

- Andy Walker

Take a snobby approach when running the numbers

While running the numbers is important and property investment should be thought of as a business, I still like to take a slightly snobby approach to any investment decisions! If the property is aesthetically pleasing relative to the area, or if it has a unique selling point (balcony, penthouse, large square footage, outdoor space), I'd prefer to invest in it and take a small hit on the returns.

Why? It's all about the exit strategy: ideally you want to be able to sell to the owner-occupier market - not just to the investor market (where you'll only achieve investor prices!).

- Christopher Browne

If you want to be hands-on, invest close to home

If you intend to be a hands-on investor, make sure you invest as close to home as possible.

Your properties should fit in with your life - they shouldn't dictate it. A property on the other side of the country might be a great deal, but do you really want to spend all your time travelling there and back?

- Neil Mansell, <u>www.thepropertyhub.net/neil-mansell</u>

On the other hand... don't be afraid to go outside your local area

It's natural to want to invest in your local area, because it's where you feel like you have the most control over your investment: if anything goes wrong, you can be there in minutes.

But if something goes wrong, do you want to be there in minutes? If you want to be a hands-on "landlord" and you enjoy fixing things, that's fine; but if you want to be an "investor", you can just employ an excellent letting agent and leave it to them. I have properties I haven't visited in years - and some investors have properties they've never visited.

Your local area is also where you feel that you know the market best, and it's true that every area has good streets and bad streets - and often good and bad sections of the same street. But in reality, that local knowledge can easily be replicated by a few weekend scouting trips plus taking advice from local experts.

My point is that there's nothing wrong with staying local (many investors build up big local portfolios and do very nicely), but there's no reason why you have to stay local if the area doesn't match your strategy. If you're living in London and investing primarily for income, for example, you could probably double your yield if you looked elsewhere.

There's a whole separate issue that comes from being willing to invest anywhere (namely: where do you invest?), but make sure you're not restricting yourself and missing out on the best investments for you just because you want the comfort of being able to pop round to pat the brickwork reassuringly whenever you want to.

- Rob Dix, www.thepropertyhub.net/rob-dix

Look at old maps of the area

If you have the address of the property you're looking to buy, visit www.thepropertyhub.net/oldmaps to view old maps of the local area. You can take a look at how the area has changed throughout history, and see when your property was built. Fascinating!

- Peter Murphy

Assume that a BTL will eat up 40% of income in expenses

When trying to figure out what a property will throw off in terms of cash flow before any debt service, assume 40% of the total gross income will be consumed for voids, maintenance, property management, letting fees and other running costs. Yes, 60% is all you will have for debt service on average.

While many landlords tend to argue with the 40% assumption, rarely do they come up with data to back up an alternative. As this is only an estimate, you do need to check the numbers per property before signing the contract. 40% is the starting point. For HMOs the costs will be higher. For new builds they might be lower.

- **John Corey, www.propertyeducation.org/john-corey**

Figure out what's available to you locally

If you're a landlord, contact your local authority to see if they have a landlord accreditation scheme (it doesn't matter if you self-manage or use a letting agent). I've received the following benefits from the scheme I belong to:

- Free gas and electrical safety certificates

- Free advertising for my rental properties

- Free credit referencing

- Energy efficiency incentives - including large discounts on boilers and radiators

- Discounts for properties in licensed areas

- A bond scheme for accredited landlords

- Mark Morris

Have a plan to add value

It's said that you make your profit when you buy, not when you sell - and if you can't achieve that by buying below market value, the alternative is to make improvements that *add* to the value of the property. (Often, of course, you'll want to buy a bargain *and* add value.)

Refurbishing a tired property is the most common way of adding value, but you can also apply techniques like extending the lease, solving a legal problem or achieving planning permission for a change of use. In every case, you're removing a problem that's holding back the value of a property and helping it to realise its full potential.

Just like buying BMV, this allows you to remortgage at the property's "new" value in the future, releasing some or all of the funds you originally put in so that you can use the same money again for your next purchase.

Without securing a bargain or adding value, you'll only be able to refinance and release your funds after the local market has gone up and raised the value of the property - which could take a lot longer than you'd like.

- **Rob Dix, www.thepropertyhub.net/rob-dix**

Double the cost and triple the time

Whether you're doing a back-to-brick development or simply budgeting for maintenance throughout a tenancy, keep this mantra in mind to ensure you don't eat into your projected cash flow and profit: "Double the cost and triple the time."

If you estimate that a refurbishment will cost £10,000, double it. It only takes an easily missed problem such as woodworm to result in a completely new kitchen.

If you reckon it'll take eight weeks - triple it. Forgot to check if it has a gas supply? Now wait up to six weeks for a new gas supply!

The end result is that you always end up under budget and on time.

If the deal stacks up even after taking the above into account, you've got a stress-free deal that won't keep you up at night.

- Nick Stott, www.thepropertyhub.net/nick-stott

Be ballsy when negotiating

Halfway through the purchase of a leasehold flat, I discovered that the estimated service charge for the following year was £25,000, split between three flats. That's £8,333 a year more than I was expecting.

I went back to the estate agent and it was news to him too. He had a chat with the seller, and then asked what I'd like to do. I decided that rather than ask for a reduction in purchase price, I wanted the seller to pay the service charge before I purchased the property. (Had I got a price reduction and paid the service charge myself, I'd have had to put in more cash.)

The vendor agreed, which surprised me: I thought he'd laugh at the idea!

Lesson learnt: be ballsy and ask for what you want - you never know what the other party might think/do.

- Kylie Ackers, www.thepropertyhub.net/kylie-ackers

Understand the benefits of being a cash buyer

Imagine you have £100,000 in cash: should you buy one property worth £100,000 outright, or split your cash pot into deposits on four properties worth £100,000 each?

Ultimately (as you'll read elsewhere in this book), as long as prices rise over the long term, the magic of leverage will allow you to do better if you take out mortgages to buy four properties. However, there are advantages to buying in cash initially then taking out a mortgage later.

Being a cash buyer puts you in a privileged position: estate agents and vendors will take you more seriously because they know your offer doesn't carry the risk of falling through as a result of struggling to obtain a mortgage. If they have multiple offers at around the same price, the cash offer will almost always be the one that's accepted.

Cash also allows you to secure discounts because of the speed at which a transaction can take place. If a vendor needs to move on quickly for some reason, guaranteed cash in the bank in a few weeks' time could be more attractive than £20,000 more in a few months.

It's not appropriate for every situation, but cash does sometimes allow you to win deals or secure discounts that wouldn't otherwise be possible. And if your bank account isn't that flush, you can also gain the same speed advantage by using a bridging loan to make the purchase, and then remortgaging later - although the cost of the loan will need to be factored in.

- **Rob Dix, www.thepropertyhub.net/rob-dix**

Find the magic mix of yield and fundamentals

Property investors are often chasing the highest yield: they want to buy a property that generates the highest amount of rent for the lowest purchase price.

But this is only part of the picture. Unlike getting 3% in one savings account rather than 2% in another (with any risks guaranteed by the government), high yield can mean high risk - or might not be so impressive once costs have been taken into account.

For example, there are many places in the country where you can buy a terraced house for less than you paid for your car - and on paper, it would achieve a yield of 12-15%. But the reason these properties are so cheap is that demand is low - meaning you could struggle to find tenants, and the tenants you do find might not take the best care of the place. By the time you've accounted for voids and high maintenance costs, that impressive gross yield could be cut down to a disappointing net return.

What's more, you're unlikely to see much capital growth on these cheap, high-yielding properties - again, because demand is low so there are no owner-occupiers driving up the prices. You'll feel smug while you're pocketing a 12% yield rather than the 8% you could have got a mile down the road, but you'll feel pretty daft in ten years when the other property has gone up in value by £50,000 while yours has remained static.

The magic combination is yield + fundamentals. It's strong fundamentals - like jobs, shops and transport links - that keep tenant demand high. And it's strong fundamentals that will give you long-term growth driven by the demand that comes from being in an area that's a good place to live. So by all means maximise the yield you can achieve - but unless it's part of a specific strategy that you've worked out, don't compromise on the fundamentals to get it.

- Rob Dix, www.thepropertyhub.net/rob-dix

Understand what BMV is... and what it isn't

Below market value (BMV) is the holy grail of property investment. But how can you actually be sure you've found a BMV property? And equally, if you're using a sourcer or property investment company, how do you know they're telling you the truth when they say they've found you a BMV property?

What BMV is not:

BMV is *not* an inflated asking price.

For example, I could offer to sell you this book for 50% off. Super generous, right? Not if my original asking price was £1,000. Even *I'll* admit that £500 for this book is a little steep!

The point is this: don't be fooled by an asking price. An asking price is just an opinion - and you need to assess for yourself whether the asking price is right.

What BMV is:

A BMV property is a property that's selling below its true value.

You can establish if a property is BMV by doing the following:

- Find out the current asking prices of similar properties in the area.

- Find out the recent sold prices of similar properties in the area.

- Talk to the local agents and see what they say (pose as a buyer and then call back posing as a seller; you may get two different numbers).

- Get your own valuation report done (it can be costly, but is probably worth it if you're still not sure about a property).

- Rob Bence, www.thepropertyhub.net/rob-bence

Consider the past, the present, and THEN the future

You're lucky to have a wealth of online resources to help with your research, so make use of these when thinking about where to buy.

For instance, has the area been a good investment in the past? Why is this - and is it likely to still be the case in the future? An area might be prosperous now because of a single employer who's increased employment - thus encouraging people to move there and spend money locally. What if that employer closed down or moved their operation elsewhere?

What timescale are you planning for your property investment? Do you believe that the area will continue to thrive for that long, or do you think that the area is up-and-coming due to a planned new train station or school?

Over the past 30 years, many towns and cities have grown and changed beyond all recognition. Some areas that were once considered slums are now where the rich and famous live. As for the area *you're* considering... what will it be like in the future?

- Graeham Broderick

Look at properties that didn't sell at auction

I've never been a fan of buying at auction, because it can involve the hard work of looking at multiple properties which all end up going beyond your maximum bid. (There's also the risk that you'll get carried away and go beyond your maximum bid yourself!)

However, it's always worth looking at the properties that didn't sell at auction - because there's a good chance that the vendor was banking on selling on that day, and will be more open to offers than they were previously. Even if they were unrealistic about the price they wanted, a room full of people refusing to match that price could make them look at the transaction in a different light.

Of course, some properties don't sell at auction because everyone's spotted something glaringly wrong with it - or it's just not an attractive property to own. But often, properties don't sell due to pure chance - maybe the auction was poorly attended, or the property was in an area far from the auction house which local bidders weren't familiar with, or the right bidder just didn't happen to be in the room.

It's also sometimes worth offering on a property you particularly like before the auction: chances are the vendor will want to wait and see if they can get a better price in the room, but occasionally someone will just want the certainty of doing the deal now.

In either case, it's likely that you'll still be required to pay the auctioneer's fees and complete within 28 days.

- **Rob Dix, <u>www.thepropertyhub.net/rob-dix</u>**

Chapter 3: Finance your investment

Stress test at higher rates of interest

Whether you're investing primarily for income or capital growth, you should never be in a position where a property is losing you money every month. It will probably increase in value eventually, but you may not have the luxury of time to find out: if something happens to your personal finances and you can't meet the mortgage payments, the property could get repossessed.

For that reason, it's important to make sure that a property will be making you money not only now, but also in the future when interest rates might be higher. So when you're considering a purchase, calculate what your monthly mortgage payments will be at a higher interest rate and only proceed if the property will still be cashflow positive. Even for a relatively modest debt of £75,000, the difference in monthly payments at an interest rate of 4% versus 7% is £187.50.

The interest rate at which you stress test is a personal choice, depending on what you think will happen to interest rates for the duration of the period for which you will be holding the property. My personal number is 8%, but for some people it might be higher.

Although interest rates have been as high as 15% in the past, there are political reasons as to why that's unlikely to happen again - and it's worth remembering that they didn't stay that high for very long. With a cash buffer, you can always afford to subsidise a mortgage for short periods of time if interest rates spike above the maximum level you were anticipating.

- **Rob Dix,** <u>www.thepropertyhub.net/rob-dix</u>

Just because you can borrow it, it doesn't mean it's a good idea

Lending criteria is set by lenders to protect lenders, NOT landlords.

Just because a lender will advance 85% LTV based on 200 times your monthly rent does not mean that it's safe to borrow at that level.

Turn the criteria on its head. Excluding the mortgage interest, what will the annual expenses be in respect of your property? Now deduct this from your annual rent. Now do this calculation: net rent divided by interest rate % (a figure you're comfortable with) = maximum borrowing. Then work out how much deposit you will need to put in and what the LTV will end up being.

Here is an example:

- Gross rent £700 pcm = £8,400 per annum

- Estimated costs (lettings, management, insurance, ground rent, services charges, maintenance, etc.) = gross rent minus 35%, e.g. £5,460 (net rent)

- Net rent divided by 7% = £78,000 (maximum

borrowing)

If I'm happy to break even at a 7% interest rate, then £78,000 is the maximum I should borrow - regardless of what the lender's criteria are.

- Mark Alexander, <u>www.thepropertyhub.net/mark-alexander</u>

Get over your fear of interest-only mortgages

For many, the dream is to pay down the mortgages on their investment properties so that they can retire with a nice stream of rental income and no worries about interest rates or the whims of lenders. And for that reason, lots of amateur investors opt for capital repayment mortgages: they know that if they make the payment every month, in 20 or 25 years they'll own the property outright.

However, interest-only mortgages give you a lot more control over your investment, and certainly don't mean that you *can't* pay off your mortgage in 20 years if that's your plan. The lower monthly mortgage payment means you make more profit, and you have full control over what that profit is used for: it could be to pay off a chunk of your mortgage when your fixed term ends, or to invest in another property if the opportunity arises.

If you have multiple properties, interest-only also means that you can take the money you're saving and target it at paying down just one of your mortgages. For future lending purposes, it's more beneficial to have one property owned "free and clear" and another with 80% borrowing than it is to have two properties with 40% borrowing.

- Rob Dix, www.thepropertyhub.net/rob-dix

Use a separate bank account for property

When you complete a tax return at the end of the year, you'll need to report your property income and expenses separately from your other sources of income. Whether you do this yourself or use a bookkeeper or accountant, it will make things much easier if you keep a separate current account for all your property transactions. Just make sure that rents come into this account, and use its debit card for any expenses you incur.

Keeping things separate will also make it easier for you to track the performance of your portfolio - both in terms of checking that rents have come in when they're due, and in monitoring whether it's making money overall. If the balance of the account is always dwindling, you'll know that something is wrong - but if it's steadily creeping up, you'll be adding to your cash buffer and will eventually be able to use it to buy another property!

- **Rob Dix, www.thepropertyhub.net/rob-dix**

Keep a healthy cash buffer

One of the most frequent questions I get from new investors is: "How much of a contingency fund should I have?"

The answer is that there's no right answer: it depends on the number of properties you have, how much maintenance they're likely to need, your attitude to risk, whether you have a rich brother-in-law who you could be sure to borrow £10,000 from in a pinch, and so on. Some investors have hard rules like "10% of the value of my portfolio" or "10% of the rent that comes in", whereas others feel comfortable with a fixed number - or don't think about it much at all.

It's galling to see a chunk of cash sitting in a deposit account when it could easily go towards buying a new property. But it's important to remember that cash is the lifeblood of any business, so if you're hit with an unexpected roof repair or a tenant stops paying the rent and you can't make your next mortgage payment, you're in a very fragile position.

To arrive at an estimate you might want to put on your misery-guts hat for a moment and think about all the things that could go wrong over the next year: which boilers could blow up, which roofs could leak, which tenants could trash the place and do a runner, and so on. Your attitude to risk will determine the worst case scenario you imagine - then just tot up what it would all cost, and keep that amount earmarked in your bank account (or ideally, in a separate account).

So there's no right answer, but there's one clear wrong answer: "Er,, con-what-gency fund?"

- Rob Dix, www.thepropertyhub.net/rob-dix

Check your financing every six months

At least once every six months, check the financing on all your properties to understand exactly where you stand.

Things change. For example, increases in property prices may mean that you could release some equity to invest elsewhere. And changes in interest rates may change the level of risk you're willing to take in your investments.

So set a date in your diary every six months where you book out a couple of hours to re-evaluate your financial position on your investment properties.

- Graham Clark, www.thepropertyhub.net/graham-clark

Have easily accessible liquid equity

Build up a portfolio with easily accessible liquid equity so that your property assets can be viewed as containing a reservoir of money to be released and restored as required.

There are many reasons why you should do this:

- Releasing equity is a quick way to obtain investment capital or working capital.

- There's no tax to be paid on releasing equity, as it is viewed as debt and debt cannot be taxed.

- Releasing equity is far cheaper than selling a house.

- There may be times when you need money quickly; this is a way to access money quickly in an emergency.

With this sophisticated approach to property ownership, a fleet of property assets can float high in the water and be well-positioned to weather the storms that might sink others beneath the waves.

- Ben Kaplinsky

Don't expect to borrow 100%

Lenders don't lend 100% unless they have more than 100% in collateral.

Think about it: why would they want to lend 100% of the deal price and at the same time have no upside? The lender doesn't get a share of the profits, so their best case scenario is that they get the interest as expected. At worst, they repossess and are looking at a loss of 20% or more from their capital.

If you want 100% for a specific deal, expect that any intelligent lender will want to see other collateral. They will want a charge on multiple properties or other ways to secure the debt, in order to protect themselves in the worst case.

If you want 100% financing for your project or deal and you don't want to put up the extra collateral, assume you need to share the profit with a joint venture investor: the investor will put in the cash that keeps the LTV reasonable, and take out a large share of the profits accordingly.

- John Corey, www.thepropertyhub.net/john-corey

Make sure your mortgage broker is experienced with property investors

Many newbie property investors use the same mortgage broker they used for buying their own home, but that could be a big and costly mistake.

Most brokers are great at handling your residential mortgage application, but dealing with buy-to-let mortgages is a completely different ball game. There are so many hoops to jump through and obstacles to avoid - and using a broker who lacks experience could cause your deal to fall over. If you're buying below market value (which you should be), deals need to happen quickly: if your mortgage doesn't move fast enough then you might lose the deal.

Make sure your broker has lots of experience working with investors (and ideally they'll do their own property investing too). A good question to ask is what percentage of their work is residential and what percentage is investment. You want the majority of their work to be on the investment side.

- Rob Bence, www.thepropertyhub.net/rob-bence

Don't overspend on refurbishments

An amazing number of investors squeeze every last pound off a property's asking price, begrudge paying a mortgage broker, even send documents by second class post to save a few pennies…then spend £100 on a bath tap when they refurbish the property.

When it comes to refurbishing a rental property, the main factors are making it clean, safe and durable. Unless you're going for the extreme high end of the market, tenants won't pay a premium because you've used Farrow & Ball paint or installed fancy LED lighting in the bathroom cabinet – so anything you spend more than what's strictly necessary will make a dent in your ROI.

If you're using a letting agent, ask them to advise you on the specification of the refurbishment: they see hundreds of similar properties every year, and they know what makes a property rent quickly at the best price and what is just unnecessary overkill. Often they'll also have relationships with suppliers who can offer you better prices on fixtures like carpets and curtains than you could find on your own.

- **Rob Dix, www.thepropertyhub.net/rob-dix**

Chapter 4: Deal with tenants and management

Avoid communicating with your tenant directly

As friendly as it may seem, it's unwise to communicate directly with a tenant if you're using an agent.

There have been many cases of landlords handing over their phone numbers to tenants "just in case", but when those landlords get woken at 3am about an alarm that won't switch off - or they get called up about a request for a rent review - everything gets a bit more difficult and muddy.

Clear and defined lines of communication are easier to manage for everyone concerned!

- Lynne Rees, www.thepropertyhub.net/lynne-rees

Build a good relationship with letting agents

I worked with my daughter to build up a £5,000 net cashflow with rent-to-rent properties in six short months. And if I had to pick just one reason why we achieved such great results so quickly (and from a standing start), I'd put it down to the good relationship we built with our letting agent.

When you're working with a letting agent and a deal comes along, be super-slick professional and preempt their every move - thereby making the process as simple as possible for them. Agents will do everything they can for friendly clients who make their lives easier!

Francis Dolley, www.thepropertyhub.net/francis-dolley

Be kind to canines - and tenants will think you're top dog

Opportunistic landlords, take note: lots of people love to own pets, but most landlords don't like renting to people with pets. As a result, there's a huge group of potential tenants who - due to the existence of a Fido, a Felix or a Fluffy - struggle to find good rental property.

Renting to a tenant with pets *can* lead to more wear and tear, yet by following these two simple steps you can reduce that risk and have tenants queuing up to rent from you:

1.   Take a larger deposit than normal, so that if the dog really does scratch the sofa (and everything else) to smithereens, you'll be protected financially.

2.   Interview the pet. Well… check the pet out when meeting your potential tenant for the first time, at least. If it's a Rottweiler whose bite is clearly worse than his bark, you can make a better-informed decision on whether or not to wait for another tenant.

- **Rob Bence, www.thepropertyhub.net/rob-bence**

Always get tenants' contact details other than mobile numbers

If you're managing the property yourself and you communicate with tenants directly, you need more than just their mobile number: it can be frustrating if you need to contact a tenant urgently and they've changed their number without telling you.

So be sure to get their email address at the very least. You could also connect with them on social media or LinkedIn.

- Mark Morris

Allow your tenant to personalise the property (within reason)

Allowing your tenant to personalise the property will encourage them to stay longer, as it will feel more like a home for them.

If they've only signed a six-month AST, however, it's wise to include a clause stipulating that no redecoration (paper and paint) can be proposed within the first 12 months of the tenancy. This is particularly useful for new builds, as you don't want someone changing the freshly painted walls to suit their style if they're then going to leave after seven months!

- Lynne Rees, www.thepropertyhub.net/lynne-rees

Don't take everything at face value

In a typical HMO there'll be so many different personalities with different life experiences - and they'll all be sharing the communal areas. Some tenants will bully, others will be victims and a few won't give a damn.

Before you jump to conclusions over who left the washing up, vomited on the bathroom floor or left the front door open after being dragged off to the police custody suite, stop and consider the options. In 99% of instances no one will admit liability, but everyone will expect the landlord to sort it out.

Learn to be a detective by interviewing, but don't get too involved. Most conflicts end up fizzling out before you've even completed the S21.

- Serena Thompson, <u>www.thepropertyhub.net/serena-thompson</u>

Insist on a thorough inventory

When renting out your property to a new tenant, don't rely on your agent to perform your inventory. From my own experiences, they can often be very vague in their descriptions.

For example, my last inventory outlined "Kitchen: pots & pans - average". This doesn't give you much to rely on when your tenant clears off with all your crockery except the frying pan.

Find the time to create a detailed inventory yourself. Then on the day that your tenant moves in, agree this with them in person and get both parties to sign. Much cheaper, much quicker and much more reliable.

- Graham Clark, www.thepropertyhub.net/graham-clark

Consider not charging a deposit

I know – not charging a deposit might seem like total madness, and in most cases it is. However, there are circumstances where *not* asking for a deposit works in everyone's favour.

As a general rule, landlords tend to ask for six weeks' rent as a deposit against damage and non-payment of bills at the end of the tenancy. The logic for six weeks is that even if the tenants do a runner and don't pay the last month's rent, you still have money left over to pay for anything that needs to be put right.

However, this can leave tenants financially stretched – especially if they're moving out of one rented home into another and needing to find the cash for another deposit before getting their previous deposit back.

An alternative is to use a specialist insurance product – often called Deposit Replacement Insurance - which pays out for anything that a deposit would usually cover. The tenant normally pays the small insurance premium. This is clearly beneficial for tenants, but there are advantages for landlords too: it saves registering the deposit with a scheme, and does away with disputes about deductions at the end of a tenancy.

In most cases I wouldn't go down this route because tenants are likely to take better care of your property if they know they're financially on the hook for any damage – and if someone doesn't have cash on hand to pay a deposit I'd be worried about them getting into financial trouble later. However, it's worth knowing about this option because there will be situations (especially at the lower end of the market) where it could be a selling point for your property and get it let faster.

- Rob Dix, www.thepropertyhub.net/rob-dix

Make sure you'd be happy to live there too

If it all went wrong tomorrow, would you be happy to move into the property yourself?

If the property isn't clean, safe and of a pleasant standard, how do you expect to find a decent tenant?

- Mark Loughnane

Choose your letting agent carefully

Whether you own a single buy-to-let flat or a portfolio of 100 investment properties, you're a business owner. And if you choose to have your properties managed, your letting agent becomes your number one employee, your marketing and advertising manager, your purchasing manager, your customer care manager, your maintenance manager and your personnel manager all rolled into one. In other words, your letting agent is the most important person in your organisation other than yourself.

There's no excuse for having a "bad" letting agent: you choose them yourself, and you likely have hundreds to choose from if your property is in a city.

As the business owner, you need to select your letting agent as you would an employee: through a vigorous and thorough selection process. If there are 200 letting agents in your city, invite them all to apply for the job! Within a day you could find all their email addresses; tell them what you're looking for and ask them how they can help you achieve your goals - and how much it will cost you.

Fifteen years ago I did just that: I wrote a polite letter to every letting agency within my target city, telling them that I intended to build a portfolio of investment properties over my lifetime. I explained that I wanted an agent to show me the very best and easy-to-let small, older properties in the best locations - properties that I could add a bit of value to. I added that I'd then hand them the keys for full management over the next 50 years.

I received just three replies. Two were very brief notes asking me to call them. I didn't bother. The third was a very well-written and helpful letter outlining what they could do for me, followed by a phone call from the boss himself. We met, discussed my plans, and I've been working with that agency ever since.

- Graeham Broderick

Plan for winter

If you're managing your own property, make sure that your tenants are well-informed about keeping pipes warmed through - even when they're not there.

Many tenants will go away to visit family over the festive period, and they'll consider it a money-saving exercise to switch the heating off. This can lead to numerous problems, including mould, burst pipes and internal leaks.

- Lynne Rees, www.thepropertyhub.net/lynne-rees

Calculate damage deductions

If damage to an item (e.g. a carpet) is so extensive that it's considered detrimental to the rentability of the property, you can make a claim against the deposit.

You won't receive the full original value of the carpet because that would be classed as "betterment": the value of most things in a rental property will depreciate with use (just like a car), and therefore a claim would only be awarded on the present value of the item.

The present value of an item is calculated as follows (with example costs to make it easier to understand):

a)   Cost of like-for-like replacement - £500

b)   Age of current item - 2 years

c)   Average expected lifespan of item - 10 years

d)   Residual lifespan (c) minus (b) - 8 years

e)   Depreciation value (a) divided by (c) - £50 per year

f)   Reasonable cost to tenant (d) multiplied by (e) - £400

- Lynne Rees, www.thepropertyhub.net/lynne-rees

Make sure your property is looked after when it's empty

Empty properties still need to be managed. So when you're choosing a letting agent, be sure to discuss what happens when there are vacancy periods: who'll visit to switch on the heating over the winter months (to ensure the pipes don't crack)? If it's a new build and there are no viewings booked, who'll call in to ensure it's well-ventilated (to prevent mould from new plaster)?

- **Lynne Rees, www.thepropertyhub.net/lynne-rees**

Get to the root cause of mould

One of the most frequently raised maintenance issues is mould. Tenants naturally assume that the property has problems with damp, but the majority of the time (except in new builds) mould is due to excess condensation.

Luckily, condensation is quite simple to control: it requires a combination of sufficient ventilation, heating and insulation, and producing less moisture in the first place:

Ventilate the property:

Condensation is caused by moisture in the air coming into contact with cold surfaces (like walls and windows), and mould then appears where there's condensation. Adequate ventilation helps the moisture-laden air escape from the home before condensation occurs.

Here are some ways to ventilate the property:

- When a room is in use, keep a small window and/or vent open (especially in kitchens and bathrooms).

- Use extractor fans.

- Do not overfill wardrobes - let the air circulate freely inside.

- Pull wardrobes and furniture away from walls, and

keep tops of wardrobes clear - again, to allow the air to circulate.

Heat and insulate the property:

Constant, low-level heating will raise the temperature of internal surfaces and prevent the rapid cooling of moisture-laden air - in turn reducing the amount of condensation.

Thermal insulation (loft or cavity wall insulation, draught-proofing and double-glazing) will help to reduce the amount of heat lost from a property - helping to maintain the constant low-level heating and keeping fuel bills down.

Produce less moisture:

Producing less moisture in the first place is a good preventative measure when it comes to mould! Here are some ways to do it:

- Washing should be dried outside the property whenever possible. Alternatively, it should be dried in the bathroom with the door closed and the window wide open.

- Tumble dryers should permanently be vented to the outside of the property.

- When cooking, pans should always be covered.

- Don't use liquid petroleum gas or paraffin heaters, as these fuels produce water vapour during combustion.

The next step is to educate your tenant into following these tips; educating them with regular emails and/or a printed document of tips is a good way to go about it.

- Lynne Rees, www.thepropertyhub.net/lynne-rees

Establish fair wear and tear

Domestic tenancies must allow for reasonable wear and tear - and no deposit claim will be upheld for minor marks to a wall or slightly dirty carpets. If, however, you feel that the attrition is excessive for the period in which the tenant has lived there, you should consider making a claim.

But where is the line drawn?

There are no precise rules on what is considered "fair wear and tear" and what is considered "damage". A good rule of thumb to follow is this: has the item been damaged or worn through natural use or sheer negligence?

Here are a few examples of the difference between "fair wear and tear" and "damage":

- If something was in good condition at the start of the tenancy but broken at the end (incurring a cost for replacement or repair), then it's considered "damage" and the tenant is liable to pay for it.

- Cleaning is never a wear-and-tear issue. If something is filthy when it was clean to start with, it should be cleaned at the tenant's cost (provided there's proof of how clean it was at the beginning).

- Light marks on the carpet are likely to be viewed as

unavoidable - i.e. "fair wear and tear".

- If appliances have broken down due to age, that's considered "fair wear and tear".

- Carpet burns, chips and cracks in baths and sinks, and broken windows all constitute damage.

- If the tenant has painted rooms in the property in a non-neutral colour without the landlord's permission, then it's considered "damage" and the cost of repainting can be charged to the tenant.

- Lynne Rees, <u>www.thepropertyhub.net/lynne-rees</u>

Credit check postcodes as well as tenants

When you take on new tenants, your letting agent will credit check them before they move in. So why not do the same when you look to invest in a new area? It's simple to do and could save you from making a costly mistake.

Checkmyfile (www.thepropertyhub.net/checkmyfile) offers a free credit-checking service for individual postcodes (click on "Check Any Postcode" at the top of the site). Simply enter the postcode and get a free report on the area.

The report gives you information including:

- Typical family composition in the area (singles, couples, families, etc.)

- Average age

- Qualifications

- Employment status

- Number of company directors

- Housing type (detached, terraced, flats, etc.)

- Newspapers read

- Amount of internet usage

It's particularly useful to do this if you're targeting a certain tenant profiles, e.g. professionals.

- Rob Bence, www.thepropertyhub.net/rob-bence

Review your own rent

A good agent should review the rent annually, but some get lazy so it's wise to set a reminder and do it yourself - just in case!

Some rental price fluctuations throughout the year are unrelated to overarching rental prices - e.g. the summer season typically sees increased demand from people looking to relocate, so rental prices increase accordingly. As a result, you're more likely to get an accurate account of *actual* rental increases by reviewing the market at exactly the same time of year, every year.

- Dale Hornidge, www.thepropertyhub.net/dale-hornidge

Write a manual for your property

I recommend giving new tenants a manual containing useful information like reliable plumbers, baby sitters, good bars and restaurants, where the local tip is, what days the rubbish and recycling are done, where the stop cock is located, etc.

The manual can easily be stored in a level arch file with plastic pockets for each section, and the tenant can add their own information too - which can then be handed over to the next tenants.

Some of your tenants may be completely new to the area, and they won't know the sorts of information that long-term residents often take for granted. Not only will the manual help them to get settled more quickly, but it also provides a nice, personal touch.

- Sheila West

Let your property unfurnished (if you have the choice)

When you let a property, the market sometimes dictates whether you let it furnished or unfurnished. For example, prime city centre apartments will often need to be let furnished to get a tenant. However, in most cases you have the option.

And if you have the option, you should let unfurnished. There are many reasons why:

- **You save money!** You don't have to buy furniture in the first place AND you don't have to keep replacing old and broken items - saving you even more money. Over time this could equate to thousands of pounds saved.

- **Your tenants are likely to stay longer.** When tenants buy their own furniture, they turn your property into their *home* - making them more likely to feel comfortable and stay longer. What's more (and as we all know when we move home), it's a huge hassle to lug furniture from one property to the next. If your tenant buys all their own furniture and knows they'll have to take it all with them when they move out, they'll be less inclined to move as quickly as if the place were fully furnished.

- **Your tenants will treat the property better.** When you let a furnished property to a tenant, they have little incentive to look after your furniture (other than the fear of losing their deposit). If they bring their own furniture, they'll take greater care of it - and greater care of your whole property in general.

So... letting your property unfurnished saves you money, keeps tenants for longer, and results in your property being left in a better condition!

- **Rob Bence, www.thepropertyhub.net/rob-bence**

Look after your boiler

There are actually two parts to this...

1.   Find a good local plumber who can be relied upon.
      Ignore Yellow Pages or Google adverts and go with
      personal recommendations only: a good indication of
      a fantastic plumber is one who doesn't need to
      advertise. The plumber may not be cheap, but paying
      a good, reasonable price is a worthwhile investment
      in peace of mind and reduced hassle.

2.   If your existing boiler is old, buy a good-quality new
      one that can easily cope with the energy demands of
      the property. Then make a maintenance/call-out
      agreement with your plumber and give their contact
      details to the tenants for emergencies.

- Tony Fulford

Do whatever it takes to minimise voids

"Voids" (a property sitting empty) is a word that sends shivers down any investor's spine: just one month of vacancy each year could wipe out a profit or put a severe dent in your net yield. The secret to a profitable property, then, is to keep voids as low as humanly possible.

The first opportunity to do this is when you're acquiring a property in the first place: see if you can get access after exchange and before completion to do any works that are needed, to reduce the amount of time that you're making mortgage payments without rent coming in. Even if you don't get permission and have to wait to do the works, you can still market the property while a refurb is happening: not all tenants will be able to see past the chaos of a building site, but many will be delighted to see that they can move into a property that is being made as good as new.

While your property is on the rental market, be sure to keep on top of your letting agent and ask for frequent updates. You don't want to cross the line into being a pest, but it's certainly true that the squeaky wheel gets the grease.

And finally, once you've got good tenants in place, make sure you hang on to them. Fix any problems quickly, and be reasonable about rent increases: if a tenant leaves when you raise the rent from £500 to £550 and it takes you a month to find someone else who'll pay that amount, it will take you nearly 11 months to get back to where you were in the first place.

- Rob Dix, <u>www.thepropertyhub.net/rob-dix</u>

Don't squeeze the rents too hard

Property is a business and should be treated as such, but it's well worth remembering that if you demand the highest rent, you'll be reducing your potential tenant pool to a minimum.

If the rent is slightly off the market rate, it could be a blessing: your tenants will be aware of this, and they'll appreciate living in your property. Rent is more likely to get paid on time, and your tenancy turnover should be lower. While it's possible that you'll make slightly less profit this way, you'll be maximising your chances of a stress-free and easy property to rent - thereby allowing you to focus your time and energy on other pursuits!

- Christopher Browne

Consider taking out rent guarantee insurance

Pretty much the worst thing that can happen to you as a landlord is to have a tenant who's not paying rent.

That's why you might want to consider buying insurance that will pay out if the tenant doesn't. Yes it's another cost, but it's a small price to pay for removing your biggest single risk. And just think: if your tenant stops paying and it takes four months to get them out and another tenant in (a pretty optimistic timescale really), can you afford to cover your mortgage and other expenses during that time?

At Yellow Lettings, we include the best possible rent guarantee as standard: your rent will be paid on the day it's due, whether the tenant pays or not. We'll continue to pay every month until the tenant leaves, and cover any legal costs too.

Not all rent guarantees are the same, so read the small print and choose the level of cover you want rather than just the cheapest. For example, it's common for policies not to pay out until the tenant is a month or two in arrears rather than straight away.

- Rob Dix, www.thepropertyhub.net/rob-dix

Get your correspondence address up-to-date

Despite there being nearly four million properties in the private rental sector, it still seems to baffle almost every property-related organisation when you have a different correspondence address from the address of the property in question. This can cause all kinds of headaches – such as bills becoming overdue and legal action being taken because they're in a stack of post that your tenant is using to prop open their bedroom door.

So when you acquire a new property, make sure your correct address details are held by:

- The council tax department of the local authority

- Your mortgage lender, if you have one

- The freeholder and management company, if the property is leasehold

- The utility companies, if you're paying for utility bills

Rob Dix - www.thepropertyhub.net/rob-dix

Chapter 5: Focus on your strategy and goals

Think about your exit from the start

You might never want to sell your properties - and there's nothing to stop you from keeping them forever and then passing them on to your children. But you never know what the future holds: there might be a time when you need to sell, when you want to free up capital for another investment, or when a property just doesn't fit in with your strategy anymore .

For that reason, even if selling isn't part of your plans, it's a good idea to think about your exit strategy before buying any particular property. In other words: if you decided you didn't want to own the property anymore, how easy would it be to sell it to someone else for a good price?

Properties that can be tricky to exit from are:

- High-rise blocks of flats, which are hard to obtain a mortgage against - meaning you can usually only sell to a cash buyer.

- Properties of non-standard construction, which again will often restrict you to cash buyers.

- Small studio flats or student pods, which you can normally only sell to other investors - who will always want a discount!

- Properties in deprived areas where there's a limited owner-occupier market, again meaning that you will have to sell to an investor.

All of these types of property might fit your strategy and generate a good yield, but before you buy consider if you're comfortable with the possible implication if the time comes to sell.

- Rob Dix, www.thepropertyhub.net/rob-dix

Remember that there's no rush

It *is* possible to make money phenomenally quickly in property - but doing so involves a phenomenal amount of effort, cash, high-risk tolerance and the odd slice of luck. For the rest of us, it's reassuring to remember that you can play the long game and still end up in a better financial position than the vast majority of the population.

A long-game strategy that I like is to get as quickly as possible to the point where your purchases are self-financing - in other words, the net rental income from your portfolio is enough for you to make regular purchases of new properties without having to put in any earned income from your job, business or personal savings.

For example, let's say you're buying houses for £100,000 by putting down a deposit of £25,000. If you and your partner have a combined income of £50,000, you'd need to live off half of your wage and put the other half into a deposit to buy one property per year. Tough, but not impossible.

But after five years of doing this, you could have five properties earning you a net income of £25,000 (assuming a net yield of 5% - again tough, but not impossible). From this point onwards, you can buy another property every year without having to put in any of your own money - and by Year 10 the net income from your properties will equal the amount you're earning in your jobs.

This is simplistic and doesn't take account of many factors, but it also involves doing nothing clever at all (if you buy below market value, add value to refinance or invest in HMOs, the numbers become even better). And the point is that you don't *need* to do anything clever: five or more years of saving hard might sound like a lot, but it's really not when it sets you up for the rest of your life.

Want to know more about playing the long game? Register your purchase of this book at www.thepropertyhub.net/tipsbonus, and we'll send you a PDF article that explains the "long game" model with more detailed workings.

- **Rob Dix, www.thepropertyhub.net/rob-dix**

Use a Dreamline to set your goals

A Dreamline is a great way to set out what you want to achieve from property and motivate you to make it happen: it encourages you to think about what your ideal life would look like, then work backwards to see how you can achieve it.

Essentially, a Dreamline is a spreadsheet that lists all the things you would want in your ideal life alongside what those things would cost you in terms of upfront cost and ongoing monthly expense. For example, if you want a fancy car, that might cost you £50,000 upfront plus £300 per month for maintenance.

You end up with your dream life fully costed out, so you know exactly how much money you need to be bringing in from property to make it happen. This target is highly motivational, because you know that if you achieve it you can have the exact life you want.

Want a free video course on goal-setting? Register your purchase of this book at www.thepropertyhub.net/tipsbonus, and you can get it! The course includes a full explanation of the Dreamlining concept and a spreadsheet that you can use to complete your own.

- **Rob Dix, www.thepropertyhub.net/rob-dix**

Develop a strategy after setting goals

If a goal is the destination, then your strategy is the road map. Few people set goals and even fewer create a strategy to achieve them - which is a shame, because the people who do so rapidly increase their success rate. (In fact, at RMP Property we won't even let anyone so much as *look* at an investment until we've helped them come up with their goals and strategies.)

So how do you do it? Goals come first: think about what you want to achieve, and be sure to make them SMART!

S: Specific. Use precise numbers and dates.

M: Measurable. Make sure your goal can be measured by asking yourself questions like "How much?", "How many?" and "How will I know when it's been accomplished?"

A: Attainable. Is your goal actually attainable, given your financial situation and options?

R: Realistic. Given your time constraints, determination and other commitments, is your goal realistic?

T: Timed. (Similar to Specific.) Without a timeframe, there's no sense of urgency.

Now it's time to think about your strategy. Talk to people more experienced than you are (The Property Hub is a good place to start!), and explain your goals so that they can help you come up with one.

Then review your strategy on a regular basis.

- Rob Bence, <u>www.thepropertyhub.net/rob-bence</u>

Focus on capital growth - not just rent

Newbies to property investment typically make the mistake of trying to become wealthy through rental profits. However, this is inefficient and hard to achieve.

Let's say you want to earn £100k each year from your property portfolio - which breaks down to £8,333 per month. How many properties would you need to invest in to realise that profit?

Using a realistic example, let's say you buy properties at £100k each, and they give you a positive cash flow of £200 per month (per property) after costs. You'd need 41 properties to hit your target - that's a lot of properties to fund (£4.1m worth) and then manage!

The people I know who've become wealthy through property have achieved it through growth rather than rental profits. Start thinking differently!

- Rob Bence, www.thepropertyhub.net/rob-bence

Chapter 6: Sort out your tax and accounts

Know when you don't need to complete a tax return

If your net annual profit is less than £2,500, you don't need to complete a tax form: simply ring up the tax office and inform them of your profit figure and they will adjust your tax code accordingly.

And if the buy-to-let is in joint names, you can split the profit (say, 50/50) to reduce the likelihood of going over the £2,500 threshold.

- Barry Mangan

Claim interest as an expense... but not too much

When you're investing in property, the interest on any capital you introduce into your property business is an allowable expense which you can use to reduce your taxable profits.

This means that if you increase the mortgage on your own home to release cash to invest with, the interest on this extra borrowing will be allowable because it's been introduced to your property business.

The interest on the mortgages for any investment properties will also be deductible. If the property increases in value and you remortgage to release more funds, the extra interest costs will still be deductible as long as you use the funds within your property business (e.g. to buy more properties). If instead you use the funds released for another purpose (like to fund your lifestyle), the amount you can deduct is capped at the value of the property when it first entered the letting market. This last point is complicated, so seek advice from your accountant if you reach a point where it's likely to apply to you.

- Iain Wallis, www.thepropertyhub.net/iain-wallis

Claim any costs incurred before you make your first investment

You don't need to own an investment property before you can start accumulating expenses to offset against tax: when you first start receiving rental income, you can claim any relevant expenses you incurred up to seven years before making your first investment.

These expenses could include travel and subsistence costs in the course of searching for your investment, as well as any professional memberships, tools and research materials.

- Rob Dix, www.thepropertyhub.net/rob-dix

Offset education costs against tax

Your property education can be offset against tax - but oddly, only if you're seen to be developing an existing skill rather than acquiring a new one.

In other words, an experienced property investor who goes on a course to learn a new strategy would be developing a skill and able to offset the cost of the course against tax. But if that same investor were to go on a short plumbing course, that would probably be seen as acquiring a new skill and therefore not be allowable.

At what point are you developing a skill rather than acquiring it? As is often the case with tax matters, there's no firm definition. As a guideline… if this is the first book you've read on the subject of property investment, perhaps buy another book or go on an inexpensive course. Congratulations - you've now acquired the skill of property investment, and anything from here on in will be allowable!

- Iain Wallis, www.thepropertyhub.net/iain-wallis

Consider the tax efficiency of buying furniture

In each tax year in which you rent out a property that's furnished, you can reduce your net rents (the total rent minus any bills you include within the rent) from that property by 10% before calculating the tax due on it.

For example, if a furnished property generates a net rent of £5,000 in this tax year, you can reduce that figure by 10% to £4,500. From there, of course, you can deduct any other allowable expenses such as mortgage interest and professional fees as you normally would.

You can't claim the cost of buying the furniture in the first place, but if it lasts for many years and you claim the deduction each year, you could come out ahead.

What counts as "furnished"? As ever, there's no firm definition: certainly more than carpets and blinds, but not everything down to knives and forks. If there are beds to sleep on and a table at which to eat, the definition of "furnished" would probably be satisfied.

- **Iain Wallis, <u>www.thepropertyhub.net/iain-wallis</u>**

Understand whether you're a property investor or trader

At its simplest, a property investor is someone who buys a property to rent out and collects the rental income, and a trader buys a property to sell on again for a profit without letting it.

Investors and traders are taxed differently. The main difference is that investors' profits incur capital gains tax whereas traders pay income tax, although there are some other differences too.

You don't get to decide whether you're a trader or investor - HMRC will take their own view. This means that if you buy a property with the intention of letting it out but a few months later have an unexpected opportunity to sell it on for a good profit, HMRC could look at your behaviour and classify you as a trader - which they're keen to do, as it usually results in more tax being paid!

How can you prove your intentions? One way is to send a note to your accountant explaining your plans, and also to keep any documentary evidence that explains why you changed course.

- Iain Wallis, www.thepropertyhub.net/iain-wallis

Don't think of an accountant as an expense

A good accountant will save you far more money than they cost you. Their knowledge of the allowances you can claim should see you paying less tax every year than you otherwise would - and in a more strategic capacity, they can make you aware of the tax implications of any major decisions you're considering.

Try to work with an accountant who's a property specialist, and ideally an investor too. This will allow them to better understand what you're trying to accomplish, and ensure that they have experience of what tax strategies have been effective for their other clients.

To keep your costs down, you can do your own bookkeeping or use a separate bookkeeper who charges a lower rate than your accountant would to do the same work.

Prefer to do it all yourself? Register your purchase of this book at www.thepropertyhub.net/tipsbonus, and you'll get access to our free tax course and spreadsheet template.

- Rob Dix, www.thepropertyhub.net/rob-dix

Shelter your profits from tax

Towards the end of each tax year in March, you should know how much profit your property business will have made after you've offset purchases, maintenance, courses, fees, travel and other legitimate costs. This profit is then added to any other income you may receive from a job or other investments - which means you'll be liable to pay up to 45% tax, depending on your tax band.

You could consider putting the profit into a pension, where it will be sheltered from any tax. This fund can then be used from the age of 55 to pay off mortgages or supplement income. It's also a great way of diversifying your investments.

- Graeham Broderick

Chapter 7: Use these tips, tricks and hacks

Learn about marketing

Learn marketing and implement marketing strategies to get people to say yes. For basics of marketing and how these strategies influence us in everyday life - but especially in sales - read the book *Influence: The Psychology of Persuasion* by Robert Cialdini (www.thepropertyhub.net/persuasion). It's very easy to read and full of excellent real-life applications.

- Simona Demkova

Develop repeatable systems

Repeatable systems are the key to freedom from your business: once you've got a system, you can pass it over to someone else to execute.

In property, systems can be anything from "how I find tenants" to "how I search for a property" to "how I furnish a room". Most investors tend to be fairly formulaic - and one obvious way of seeing this is to look inside their properties and notice that the carpets, curtains and furniture are often the same in every house. There's a reason for this: for each refurb they can say to their tradesperson "Same as last time please," and forget all about it.

Systems are no good if they're trapped inside your head - so next time you perform a routine task, write it down step by step. Once you have a few related tasks, you can pay someone else to execute the systems for you. You might be surprised how cheaply you can save hours and hours of your time.

You can use any method at all to write down your systems, but a good solution is Sweet Process (www.sweetprocess.com): it forces you to use an easy-to-understand step-by-step format, and you can even include pictures and screenshots.

- Rob Dix, www.thepropertyhub.net/rob-dix

Join LNPG

LNPG is a club that negotiates serious discounts with suppliers for all sorts of different materials - from kitchens and bathrooms to double glazing, paint and furnishings. The discounts are often even better than the trade gets, and LNPG achieves this by using the purchasing power of their combined membership to drive great deals. In return, landlords pay an annual membership fee - think the Costco model and you're not far off.

They also offer great deals on insurance, and I save more than the annual membership fee on buildings insurance alone. If you don't save more than the value of your membership fee, they promise to roll over your membership for another 12 months for free. There's little to lose, and potentially a lot to gain if you're planning any kind of refurb.

As a buyer of this book, you can save 10% on your LNPG membership! Just visit www.lnpg.co.uk and add **RD10** in the "affiliation code" box during the sign-up process.

- **Rob Dix,** www.thepropertyhub.net/rob-dix

Use HelloSign to sign digitally

When someone emails you a document to sign, it's a huge pain to print it out, sign it, scan it back in and return it to the sender. And because it's such a pain, if you send an important document to someone else to sign (like an inventory or tenancy agreement), they might not get around to signing it - causing you big problems down the line.

The answer is to use a digital signing service like HelloSign (http://hellosign.com). With HelloSign you can store a digital copy of your signature by scanning it in, or even just draw a signature using your mouse - it's still legally binding in the EU. You can then easily add your signature to any document, and send that document to others for their signature if needed. Better yet, if the other person *doesn't* sign the document, they'll be automatically reminded every few days until they do.

Once everyone has signed, you get emailed a definitive copy of the document with all signatures for you to file away. Easy!

- Rob Dix, www.thepropertyhub.net/rob-dix

Use block viewings to generate urgency

When trying to rent or sell a property, try to arrange group viewings to generate a sense of urgency. Alternatively, you could schedule private viewings one after the other as a less obvious way of showing there is competition for the property.

- **Tom Mannifield**

Use Evernote to digitally store documents

As soon as you own a property, you'll get all kinds of people attempting to bury you in pieces of paper - from the local council to your mortgage lender to your managing agent. However much you ask to be sent statements and notices digitally, you'll still get documents thudding onto your doormat on a regular basis.

The best thing you can do with them is to get them into Evernote - a free piece of software that allows you to store any kind of note and access it on pretty much any device. You don't need a scanner: just taking a photo on your phone will do the job.

Evernote has many great features, but the one I find most useful is that it takes a photo or a scan and extracts all the text to make it searchable. That means that if you need to find some random piece of information like your mortgage account number or the balance of your council tax account last November, you can just search "mortgage account" or "council November" and it will pull it out for you. So much quicker than leafing through all the sheets of paper in your desk drawer.

Want to learn how to use Evernote to run your property business more efficiently? Register your purchase of this book at www.thepropertyhub.net/tipsbonus and you'll get access to our course!

- Rob Dix, www.thepropertyhub.net/rob-dix

Set up Rightmove alerts

You're not a true property obsessive unless you spend more time on Rightmove than most people do on Facebook, but you still might not be using it as efficiently as you could.

Rightmove allows you to set up sophisticated filters, and you can then choose to get new properties matching those filters sent to you on a daily or weekly basis. Not only can you specify things like the price range and number of bedrooms, but you can even draw out a specific search area on the map rather than rely on a postcode - which is perfect, because so many cities have very specific "good areas" and "bad areas" that are more granular than the first part of a postcode.

Want to put automation on steroids? Register your purchase of this book at www.thepropertyhub.net/tipsbonus, and we'll show you how to feed your Rightmove alerts into a system that makes it easy for you to keep track of which properties you want to view, as well as add notes and track follow-ups.

- Rob Dix, www.thepropertyhub.net/rob-dix

Find properties to renovate (really easily)

If you're on the lookout for a refurbishment project, www.propertytorenovate.co.uk will save you from looking through endless Rightmove photos trying to work out where there's scope to make some improvements.

The site uses clever algorithms to search for phrases like "in need of modernisation" in Rightmove and Zoopla listings, and brings them all into one place - from where you can click through to view the original listing.

It's not perfect - there are some false matches, and it's not going to identify absolutely everything - but it can be a good starting point when you're just setting out to see what potential there is in an area.

- **Rob Dix, www.thepropertyhub.net/rob-dix**

Use Property Bee to learn about the history of a property

An estate agent will always tell you that every property is in high demand, and that the vendor will only sell for the right price. But are they telling the truth? You can cut through the spin and get the facts on any property by using Property Bee (www.thepropertyhub.net/propertybee) - a plugin for Firefox.

Property Bee keeps track of the history of a Rightmove listing and adds extra information into the page - including any changes to the description, and a timeline of changes in price and sale status. It all happens automatically, so all you need to do is browse Rightmove as normal and you'll see the extra information as long as you have the plugin installed.

What does this mean? If the price has just been cut by £10,000, it might imply that the vendor is getting desperate and would be open to an offer.

Get help with Property Bee! Installing Property Bee isn't the most straightforward process, so register your purchase of this book at www.thepropertyhub.net/tipsbonus, and we'll send you a video that walks you through it step by step!

- Rob Dix, www.thepropertyhub.net/rob-dix

Schedule important recurring dates with Google Calendar

There are all sorts of dates in property that are worth keeping track of, including some that could land you in big trouble if you forget them - like when a gas safety check is due, or your insurance needs renewing.

The stress-free way to remember these dates is to enter them into a digital calendar - and my favourite is Google Calendar. Just pop in an appointment for the date in question, and ask it to send you a reminder: you can choose to be reminded by email or text message with however much notice you want. You can even set up recurring reminders - so as your insurance will expire on the same day every year, you can just set a recurring annual reminder once and you'll never forget it again.

You can use reminders to make sure you're being proactive rather than reactive, too. For example, you can remind yourself on 1st November every year to schedule some preventative winter maintenance like clearing out the drains and gutters.

- Rob Dix, www.thepropertyhub.net/rob-dix

Register your copy of this book to get our bonus resources!

Now you've read the book, just visit
<u>www.thepropertyhub.net</u>/<u>tipsbonus</u> to collect the FREE bonus
resources that will help you put these tips into action:

- A 20-minute secret audio recording with more of our
  best personal tips

- Access to our FREE video courses on setting goals,
  paying less tax, saving time with efficient systems,
  and more!

- A Twitter list of our favourite property people to instantly start your property network

- Our guide on how to set up your own accountability group to make sure you hit your property goals

- A guide to show you how to automatically receive new episodes of our podcasts - more than an hour of free education every week

To instantly download all this and more, just visit www.thepropertyhub.net/tipsbonus.

Also by Rob Dix...

Property Investment for Beginners

Over 70 five-star reviews on Amazon!

This short book covers the big questions you should be asking yourself before you so much as glance at an estate agent's window. It contains jargon-free explanations of basic investment principles, summaries of the major post-crunch investment strategies, and advice on developing a mindset that will support your long-term success.

You'll learn...

- How to pick an investment strategy that matches your skills and goals

- The only three calculations you need to know to size up any deal

- An overview of every major investment approach, from the most boring to the probably-not-a-good-idea-but-here-you-go-anyway

- How to (safely and sustainably) stretch a limited pot of cash to build whatever size portfolio you want

Buy on Amazon now: www.thepropertyhub.net/pifb

Beyond The Bricks: The inside story of how 9 everyday investors found financial freedom through property

An Amazon #1 best seller

"Put this on your list of property must-reads" – Property Tribes, Book of the Month

What does it take to be successful in property investment? How can you start with nothing but a very ordinary level of savings, and amass a portfolio that means you'll never need to work for anyone else again?

Beyond the Bricks is a window into the lives of 9 UK-based investors who've done exactly that. Through long-form interviews with them we learn exactly how they did it, what their lives are like now, and what they recommend to anyone just starting out.

This book is less of a "how to" than a "how you could". It won't give you one formula for success, but many practical ideas and inspiring examples that you can use to craft your own property investment story.

Buy on Amazon now: <u>www.thepropertyhub.net/btb</u>

13611480R00088

Printed in Great Britain
by Amazon.co.uk, Ltd.,
Marston Gate.